Surviving
SEXUAL
ABUSE

DEIRDRE WALSH
ROSEMARY LIDDY

First published in 1989
2nd Edition 1993

Attic Press
4 Upper Mount Street
Dublin 2

British Library Catalogue in Publication Data
Liddy, Rosemary
  Sexual abuse handbook
  1. Children. Sexual abuse by adults
  I. Title I. Walsh, Deirdre
  367.7'044

ISBN 0-946211-61-2

Cover Design: Brenda McArdle
Printing: Guernsey Press Ltd.

SURVIVING SEXUAL ABUSE

ROSEMARY LIDDY AND DEIRDRE WALSH

Attic Press
Dublin

The case histories in this handbook are based on fact but names used are entirely fictitious.

CONTENTS

PREFACE

Child sexual abuse is now being recognised all over the world as a reality that must be faced. Over the past decade information regarding the incidence and extent of the problem has mushroomed. While studies vary in their findings, conservative estimates indicate that one in ten people experience some form of sexual abuse in their childhood.

Attempts are now being made to respond to children who have been sexually abused. Public awareness has helped many children to come forward with their abuse, and help is available both from statutory agencies and other bodies. While better services need to be provided, particularly in the area of therapy, there is at least an attempt being made to address the needs of sexually abused children. But what of the adults within our society who have been abused in their past? Sexual abuse is not a new problem — the result of a more permissive society, video nasties, pornography. It is an age-old problem. Disclosure rates in Ireland are rising year by year as victims of past sexual abuse come forward to seek help. While this handbook is primarily intended for women who have been abused as children and teenagers, it may also interest anyone working in the counselling of adults who have been sexually abused.

In this handbook we attempt to outline the complex ways in which sexual abuse can affect a woman's personality and life. Many women have arrived at a point where they realise that the price paid for secrecy is too high — and that they deserve a better quality of life, not overshadowed by the past. We hope that many more women will come to this decision after reading *Surviving Sexual Abuse*.

Perhaps the most sensitive issue to be faced in this handbook is the fact that women too have sexually abused their children. This is an especially difficult issue for women because it challenges the ideas we have of women as nurturers and caregivers. It is sadly true that an increasing number of women (and men) are beginning to disclose sexual abuse by their mothers. However it is only by recognising it as a reality, and responding, that it will change.

The cycle of sexual abuse must stop. One of the ways in which that may come about is by breaking the secrecy and the collusion around abuse. No child should be subjected to sexual abuse and no adult should have to live a life that is overshadowed by its effects. Everyone who has been abused deserves the chance of recovery. We hope that this handbook will be a source of hope and practical help for women who have been abused, and for those working with them.

CHAPTER 1

WHAT IS SEXUAL ABUSE?

SUSAN

Susan is the younger of two daughters in a family of five. The family is a happy one, well-liked in the neighbourhood; all the family would describe themselves as close. However, there is a secret. When Susan was approximately three years of age, she remembers her father beginning to touch her in a 'funny' way. He would rub her and cuddle her, but it made her feel a bit 'shivery'. Susan did not really mind as she was very fond of her father, who always told her how much he loved her. She was his special girl. Gradually, as the months went by, Susan's father started touching her genitals and making her touch his penis, but she quite liked him touching her, it felt sort of nice and anyway, she often got sweets or money for letting him. This became part of Susan's everyday life. She did not tell anyone because daddy said it was their secret. Susan did not want him to give the sweets to anyone else. However, daddy started asking her to do some very strange things. Things like putting his penis in her mouth. She thought this was awful, it was too big and made her feel like choking. Susan did not like the 'stuff' that came out of it either. But, when she refused to do it, her daddy would get really cross and say he would tell her mum that she had been bold and dirty for years. No one would believe what she said, everybody would hate her. Susan did what she was told. From seven to fifteen, Susan's father made her do worse and worse things. He had sexual intercourse with her, sometimes he even put his penis in her bottom which hurt a great deal. She grew to hate her father but she felt so disgusting she never plucked up the courage to tell anyone. When she was fifteen, she got her periods and her father said from now on it had to stop because she might get pregnant. Susan did her best to forget it had ever happened.

ANN

Ann was an only child of five years of age, loved and cared for by her parents. They went out once a week, and their next-door neighbour's son, Peter, used to babysit. He was seventeen. Ann was fond of Peter. He would play with her and read her stories. One night, as he was reading her a story and tucking her into bed, he put his hand under her night-dress and started gently to rub her legs, bottom and genitals. This happened several times, then one evening he asked if he could look between her legs. He then started to kiss Ann's genitals and lick them. Ann thought it was a dirty thing to do, she did not like it. Peter never hurt her physically but she wished it would stop. He told her it was their little secret and that her mammy would not like to know about it, it would be better not to tell her. Then one day Peter tried to put his fingers into Ann's vagina. She screamed and cried and cried. Peter comforted her and promised never to touch her again. So the abuse stopped. Sometimes Ann wished that she could have told her mammy what had happened, but she was afraid in case her mother told her she was a dirty, bad girl. After that she was always afraid of boys or men with red hair.

Child sexual assault is any exploitation of a child under the age of sixteen for the sexual pleasure and gratification of the adult. This ranges from obscene telephone calls, indecent exposure and voyeurism such as watching a child undress to fondling, taking pornographic pictures, intercourse or attempted intercourse, rape, incest or child prostitution. It may be a single incident or events which occur over a number of years. (Keeping Safe — A Practical Guide to Talking with Children, Michele Elliott, 1988, New English Library).

Sexual abuse is always an abuse of power. The power may be used in an overt (bullying) way or covert (bribing) way. Children are never in a position to give their informed consent because they do not have a mature understanding of sexuality. Most of us were told as children not to talk to strangers, especially strange men, and at one time it was thought that this was where the greatest danger lay. However as more people began to talk about sexual abuse, it became a clear fact that most victims are abused by people known to them — relatives, neighbours, friends etc, — and abuse within the family is all too common. While children are warned about men, as we learn more about sexual abuse it is clear that some children have also been abused by women. Where a woman has abused it is generally within the family. This can be the hardest type of abuse to disclose and confront.

More and more women are now coming forward with their own stories of sexual abuse. Some of these have suffered 'once off' incidents, many more have had to endure months or years of abuse. They all have one thing in common: at the time they were being abused they did not have the capacity to stop it. They were either threatened, sworn to secrecy, bribed, or coaxed into not telling. A primary factor of the abuse is that the secret is understood even if it is not talked about. For some people sexual abuse can become part of their daily lives, it goes on for so long. Many children feel that this is happening to everyone else too, it is just not talked about. Sometimes the abuse can be cruel and violent, but it can also be accompanied by apparent love and affection which makes it even harder for a child to make sense of what is taking place.

'I love my daddy, but I do not like the awful things that he does to me.' Children who are abused feel that the sexual abuse is a usual part of parental love. Often they are made to feel very special by the abuser, given special attention and time. Sometimes indeed the person who has abused them can also be the only person they ever felt loved by. In many cases, the abuse can start in infancy and continue right through to adulthood.

Even now people would like to think that abuse only happens in certain 'problem' families, but this is certainly not the case. Abuse happens in all kinds of families — 'problem' ones, happy ones, rich and poor ones.

SO WHAT DO WE MEAN BY ABUSE?

Watching and Looking
The abuser makes a child look at pornographic movies or books or makes the child watch him masturbate, or engage in other sexual activities. Sometimes the child is made to do things to themselves or with other people, so the abuser can watch them.

Kissing

The abuser kisses a child in a sexual way. Open-mouthed or french kissing are the most common, or the abuser may kiss other parts of the child's body in a sexual way.

Genital Touching

A child is made to touch or rub the abuser's genital area or to masturbate the abuser. It is also common for the abuser to touch the genital area, rubbing the child's vagina or inserting fingers into the child's vagina or rectum.

Oral Sex

Oral sex is very common in sexual abuse. The child is either made to perform oral sex on the abuser, or the abuser performs oral sex with the child. This can be the most terrifying abuse for a child because it can bring with it fears of choking to death when a penis is pushed back into the throat, or the abuser ejaculates. Children as young as six months have been subjected to oral sex.

Intercourse

'Dry intercourse' is when the abuser rubs his penis against the child's genital area, inner thighs or bottom. This can gradually progress to full vaginal and anal intercourse. The latter case occurs when the penis is inserted into the anus or rectum.

When a child is being abused for a number of years by the same abuser, it is not uncommon for the abuse to begin with kissing and genital touching, and eventually progress to oral sex and full intercourse. However, sometimes a child's first experience of sexual abuse is full intercourse and this can happen with a child as young as two or three years or even younger.

Children who are abused over a period of time can also learn to respond sexually to being touched, caressed and kissed. They may even have orgasms. People need to understand that our bodies may respond sexually even when our mental or emotional response to the abuse is very different. This can later lead to a lot of guilt and shame for those who have been abused.

As they grow older they think that they have no right to feel bad about the abuse, as they responded and 'co-operated' with it. Occasionally they may even feel that they caused it and were responsible for the abuse. *The abuser is always responsible for sexual abuse no matter what the child does or does not do.* You may be reading this and thinking 'Well, I was abused and it wasn't as bad as all that. I have no right to feel as bad as I do or to seek help now'.

There are no rules about right and wrong feeling when it comes to your abuse. What is extremely traumatic for one person can be much less so for someone else at the time. Sometimes a so-called 'minor' incident of abuse can be as devastating as full intercourse and can have a lasting effect on the person. If you have been abused and are feeling bad about it, never discount it as being too trivial to need help. The severity of abuse cannot be measured objectively because sexual abuse is always a violation of who you are as a person and it hurts you at a very deep level.

CHAPTER 2

THE EFFECTS OF SEXUAL ABUSE

BETTY

Betty is forty-six years of age, happily married with three children, twin boys of nineteen and a girl of sixteen. She and her husband get on well, they have no financial worries, they live in a lovely house. Betty works for charity, and is now raising money for cancer research. She is also involved with several local community groups. On the outside everything looks fine; the only indication that anything might be wrong is Betty's weight problem. Over the years, she has battled to keep her weight under control, going on numerous diets, but after each diet the weight piles on again during one of Betty's binges. She now weighs fifteen stone and has more or less given up. Betty and her husband do not have sex any more. She cannot bear him to see her naked, much less touch her. Sometimes she wishes he would have an affair, then she would not feel so guilty. While they do not fight and appear to get on well, there is a depressing routine about their life together, the spark and hope of the earlier years are gone. Betty never voices any of this, in fact she voices very little. She cannot bear emotion of any kind, hates to see people cry and would never cry herself. She does not feel especially close to her children, she does not really feel especially close to anyone. Sometimes Betty wonders if it should be otherwise but she does not allow herself to think about this for long.

Eight years earlier, Betty attempted suicide. Her husband came home one night to find her unconscious and her wrists bleeding badly. She was hospitalised for six weeks. During that time the psychiatrist tried to get her to talk, but she would not say why she did it. She said that she did not know, she and her husband never talked about it. Betty is locked in a lonely prison of silence; she can manage her life, provided that there is no major challenge. She does not really know herself, but she no longer wants to. She tried to look once and what happened scared her too much. Betty was abused by her brother from the age of seven to eleven years. He raped her repeatedly in her own bed late at night while her parents slept. Two weeks ago Betty decided to go for sexual abuse counselling. That was the first time she had ever told the truth about what happened to her.

The effects of child sexual abuse can be divided into two main categories: Short term and Long term.

Short Term Effects

Short term effects can also be the indicators of sexual abuse. There are those which are evident at the time of the abuse or in the days, weeks or months following an abuse or series of abuses. As short term effects can often be identified around the time of the abuse, they can be very helpful in preventing further abuse.

Typically, a sexually abused child may show some or many of the following symptoms. Some are clearly medical while others are emotional or behavioural.

Medical Symptoms include:
- Venereal disease or infection
- Teenage pregnancy
- Vaginal or rectal bleeding
- Vaginal or rectal itching or soreness
- Recurrent urinary tract infections

These are very clear signs of distress which in a child or teenager should never be left unexplained. When these kinds of symptoms are present, sexual abuse must be seriously considered, even if a child is not disclosing abuse.

Emotional or behavioural symptoms include many signs of distress that parents will often note in their children for a variety of reasons. They do not necessarily mean that your child is being sexually abused, but it is important to keep it in mind when considering other possibilities.

Fear

A child may start to show a lot of fear about men in general, or a particular man or place. This should not be ignored and it is important to check with your child why she is afraid.

Unhappiness

A child may seem unhappy and sad for no apparent reason. The child may be insecure, quiet and disinclined to mix with other children in an easy, relaxed manner. A child may even seem older than her years and unable to enjoy the things that other children enjoy. While there may be several reasons for this type of behaviour, sexual abuse may be one of them.

Behavioural Changes

A child's personality can change quite suddenly and noticeably. She may switch from being a happy, carefree and open child to being quiet, withdrawn and secretive. She may become 'too good' or fearful in a way which is not a typical feature of her personality. Alternatively, a child may suddenly become particularly bold, demanding and angry.

Night Disturbance

Night behaviour and sleep patterns may change in various ways. This can range from not wanting to sleep alone, starting to bedwet and frequently having nightmares. These are all signs of distress and should be thoroughly checked out. A stronger indication would be if a child starts suffering from night terrors which involve screaming or crying in her sleep. It is often difficult to waken a child from this type of nightmare. She may even say something like 'go away' or 'leave me alone'. These nightmares can happen to a child when she is very frightened of the abuse or the abuser. Night terrors should never be ignored.

School Performance

Sometimes the first place where a child will show evidence of distress is in school. A child's school performance may disimprove or her ability to concentrate deteriorate. A child may suddenly become apprehensive and hesitant about undressing in school for a sports class.

LONG TERM EFFECTS

Long term effects are those which may have started at the time of the abuse or may develop in the months and years following the abuse. Long term effects usually occur as a result of the person who has been abused never having spoken about it or not being believed or helped if she did. She goes on with her life, keeping this secret which may have disastrous effects on her life and personality. Some long term effects can be very serious, where the woman in an effort to keep the memories blocked becomes very self-destructive.

Alcoholism and Substance Abuse

A woman who has been abused may attempt to destroy herself through alcohol and substance abuse in an effort to escape the negative feelings she has about herself and her life. Substance abuse may include addiction to prescribed drugs such as tranquillisers or sleeping tablets.

Anxiety and Panic Attacks

A woman may constantly suffer from her 'nerves', or have very frightening panic attacks for no reason. Panic attacks can make people feel as if they are going to faint or cannot breathe. Their heart is beating fast and they are afraid of dying of a heart attack. There appears to be no logical reason for this when it is happening.

Phobias

Being terribly afraid of something for no valid reason, eg going outside the house or being in confined spaces. Some women switch from one phobia to another — one month afraid of spiders; the following month, of men with glasses.

Eating Disorders

These include Anorexia and Bulimia. Anorexia is virtually starving yourself to death and still feeling fat and ugly. Bulimia means eating huge amounts of food at a time, then feeling guilty and perhaps afterwards making yourself vomit.

Hypochondria

When a woman suffers from one illness after another, unexplained aches and pains, headaches, rashes, stomach pains etc; there is always something wrong with her and her main topic of conversation may be her various illnesses.

Prostitution

A woman who has been sexually abused may turn to prostitution. This may be partly as a result of having such negative feelings about herself that she doesn't care what she does with her body. Or she may feel that at least this time she is getting paid for the services her body provides.

Sexual Problems

Feelings about sex may be very confused or sometimes extreme. Some women may hate sex and get no enjoyment from it, going to great lengths to avoid it. Other women become sexually very active, yet often appear to get very little enjoyment from it. Some women may even feel that it is expected of them to offer sex all the time, that they have no right to say no to sex. We discuss sex and sexuality in more detail in Chapter 8.

Relationships/Trust

Most women who have suffered sexual abuse find it difficult to trust other people, particularly men. Some will not trust anybody as a result of their experiences. This makes it extremely difficult for them to form close relationships with either women or men, although this may be precisely what they want and need the most.

Guilt and Self-Esteem

A woman may feel very guilty about the sexual abuse she has suffered, convinced that it must have been her fault or that something about herself must have caused it to happen. Often this leaves her feeling bad about herself, even in situations where she has suppressed any recollection of the abuse, so she may have no idea why she feels this way. She would see herself as 'dirty', 'bad', unliked, unloved, unlovable. Many women also describe feeling as if other people know that they have been abused just by looking at them Where memory of the abuse is not clear, a woman cannot understand her own feelings and can have an unconnected sense of happiness being just around the corner, yet always out of reach.

Women who have been subjected to abuse may block their emotions and feelings. They seem to live their lives without ever really connecting to deeper feelings within themselves. This in turn limits their capacity to relate to other people in relationships at a deeper level.

Depression

This is a big problem for many women who have been abused and is generally caused by a combination of the effects we have mentioned. For some it is an anger turned in against themselves, so severe that it causes them to feel that life is not worth living, and may impel them towards suicide. Others may display depression in a 'learned helplessness', where they feel that they have no control over their lives, yet are unhappy about this state of affairs. However, they will probably do nothing to try and change it, having grown accustomed to powerlessness or being out of control.

Sexuality

Most women who have been sexually abused will experience some difficulties with their sexual identity and its expression. This is discussed in Chapter 8.

Self-Destructive Tendencies

Sometimes women who have been abused continue to abuse themselves in various ways. They may feel so bad, hopeless and despairing at a deep level within themselves that they become self-destructive in the way they live their lives. This may show itself in alcohol/substance abuse, prostitution, anorexia/bulimia, or in repeated suicidal attempts. Sometimes women actually mutilate themselves, or become obsessed with the idea of doing so.

CHAPTER 3

WHY SEEK HELP?

GERALDINE

Geraldine is thirty-two years of age. She works as a nurse in a local hospital. She has been married for four years and has no children. She and her husband get on very well. They did not have sex before they got married because Geraldine did not want to. Their honeymoon was a big strain as she hated the idea of being seen naked and of having intercourse. She thought sex would get easier as time went on but it has not. Geraldine never enjoys sex and only does it to please her husband.

About ten months ago her father died, he was sixty-three. Geraldine has never been especially close to him, but after he died she found that she could not get over her grief. She became more and more depressed, cried a lot, lost interest in her job and everything at home. Everyone she talked to said that it would take time and that it was normal to feel this way, but Geraldine knew that it was not normal. She had also begun to feel afraid and panicky. One day at work, she felt dizzy and thought that there was no breath coming into her body, her heart was thumping and she thought, 'I am having a heart attack'. These panic attacks continued and in the end her doctor prescribed tranquillisers. She could not get her father out of her mind, she kept on seeing his face and feeling afraid. There was something familiar about the fear, but she did not understand it. One night, she had a terrible nightmare and woke up trembling and terrified. She had dreamed that she was a little girl in her bed at home. There was a man leaning over her, telling her to stay quiet and be a good little girl. The man, her father, had his penis out and was holding it against her face.

She did not tell anyone about the dream. Three weeks later, when she and her husband were having intercourse, she had a flashback. Geraldine remembered being small, and a heavy weight on top of her and a hot burning sensation between her legs. She screamed at her husband and sat up shaking and frightened. Finally, she managed to tell him what was wrong. She broke down, cried and said, 'I think that my father abused me'.

Many women who have been sexually abused want to forget all about it, put it in the past and get on with their lives. Like all painful experiences, women want to move away from the hurt and sadness and live a 'normal' life again. One of the most common ways for a woman to cope with abuse is to repress or block out most of the abuse or minimise what happened, telling herself, 'well, it only happened a few times' only to discover later that her father had indeed abused her. All this denial and forgetting is a commonplace way of coping with an extremely painful experience. For many women it is often, initially, the only way. However, abuse is always buried alive. Unlike many other experiences it does not get easier with time, it does not fade or disappear. Buried with the abuse are all the feelings that surround it — sadness, fear, anger, guilt and pain. Although the memory of the abuse may be repressed, it continues to affect you and how you live your life. Some women manage to achieve much in their lives, doing well at work, raising families and enjoying all the things we usually enjoy, but there is often a persistent sense that all is not quite right, a feeling of unease and underlying anxiety. Most women who have been abused and have tried to put the abuse behind them eventually arrive at a point in their lives when they know that they just cannot go on trying to pretend that everything is alright, when it clearly is not. This can happen a few months after the abuse has stopped, or years afterwards, as many as ten, twenty or even thirty years later. There are many different catalysts that can bring on a crisis, where you finally say 'Yes, I was abused and I can no longer pretend that I was not. I need to do something about it'.

These catalysts or triggers are many and varied and what affects one woman may mean nothing to someone else, but let us look at some of the more common ones. Relationship problems which persist can often have a triggering effect. Some abused women find it hard to have close personal relationships; they find it hard to trust and to love and also to be loved. Very often a crisis within a relationship can bring a woman to a point where she is willing to acknowledge that she must look at her sexual abuse. This is especially common in marital relationships. What appears to be a marital problem is sometimes revealed as being rooted in an experience of sexual abuse. Again, it is possible for a woman to 'bury' abuse so well that she can have good relationships for many years before things start to go wrong.

Within the parent-child relationship lots of things can happen to trigger memories, eg pregnancy or the birth of a child — especially the birth of a girl. The discovery that your own child has been sexually abused can also rekindle memories of abuse. Sometimes women will speak of feeling especially protective of one particular child for no obvious reason. On deeper exploration, it emerges that a mother was abused when she was the same age as her daughter is now.

'She reminds me of when I was that age and I feel so afraid for her, I do not know why.' Sometimes a mother's relationship with her sons can trigger memories of abuse. A mother may experience a sense of fear or unease with her sons, particularly as they progress towards puberty and sexual maturity. Some women have sought help for sexual abuse following an abortion. The emotional ordeal of an abortion and subsequent thoughts of having hurt a child can awaken memories and feelings of having been deeply hurt in their own childhood.

The death of an abuser often has a strong triggering effect. This can be for many different reasons. A woman may be surprised that she does not feel upset or sad when someone dies, often there is a sense of relief or even anger. These feelings do not make sense, but probing can reveal sexual abuse, well buried and hidden away. The trauma of death has a way of lowering our defences and making us more aware. If an abuser dies, it can free women to acknowledge and track down the abuse. Women can be very torn in their loyalties, especially if they have been abused by someone by whom they have felt loved. Often they feel it would be a betrayal of the person if they talked about the abuse but when that person dies it is something of a relief.

Other women are not aware at a conscious level that this is what is happening. Women sometimes have a strong reaction of sadness, a prolonged grief reaction after the death of an abuser. In a similar way, the death of a mother can also free a woman to acknowledge and talk about sexual abuse. A woman may have kept silence for many years in order to protect her

24

mother from reality. Sometimes memories of past abuse are only uncovered while working through bereavement and grief. It is important for a woman to realise that if she has been abused, she always has the right to talk about the abuse no matter how hard that may be; she is not betraying by telling. A woman has the right to tell and the right to be helped in repairing the damage caused by sexual abuse.

As we have said, one of the possible effects of sexual abuse is substance addiction, to alcohol or drugs for example. For some, the first time that they recognise they have been sexually abused is during an addiction treatment programme. Alcohol or drugs have enabled them to deny or evade the reality for a long time and once these props are taken away, they come face to face with whatever they have been trying to avoid.

There is a strong link between sexual problems and sexual abuse. Some women who have been abused always have problems with sex, others may have positive sexual experiences for a time and only much later run into difficulties. A common experience is a flashback during sex. A woman will suddenly remember and re-experience the abuse. Specific sexual practices, eg oral sex, being touched in a certain place or in a certain way, can trigger memories of abuse. These memories can be very frightening and distressing. Young teenagers will often tell of their abuse when they first receive sex education or when they begin to develop sexually. They then realise that the abuse was not normal and should not have happened. Some sexually abused women live ordinary non-problematic lives for many years. Occasionally, they may have a vague sense that something bad happened long ago, but they manage to push it away. It can happen that at a certain stage in their lives this feeling gets stronger. This is much more likely to occur during times of stress and major change. This feeling may be accompanied by other symptoms such as panic attacks, night sweats, bad dreams, nightmares, depression or terrible fear. It is sometimes not until a crisis like this that a woman will finally face the fact that she has been abused. It becomes more difficult for women to hide from their abuse when their secret is out. Handbooks like this, TV/radio programmes, newspaper articles, are constant reminders of the fact that sexual abuse is no myth, that it does not have to be a secret any more, you have the right to tell and the right to seek help.

CHAPTER 4

WHO SHOULD SEEK HELP

ANN

Ann is twenty-eight and has two children aged eight and five years. She was sexually abused by her father and two brothers while growing up. In many ways, the only reason she married so young and so quickly was to get away from home. She could not see any other way except through marriage. At first, there were no problems. Having a home, husband and child kept her busy, and she was able to push the problem of sexual abuse to the back of her mind. She felt that from now on things would be different. However, with the birth of her second child, things started to go downhill. She was no longer content with her situation. Her husband seemed to be out more and more, he started to increase his intake of alcohol. Ann and her husband started to spend more and more time fighting, and seemed to have less in common every day. She began to wonder who she really was as a 'person'. She thought about her marriage and asked herself if this was all there was to life. Gradually, memory of the sexual abuse started to come back. Ann had nightmares about it, she found it really difficult to be with her family. Even during the day, it seemed to be at the edge of her mind at all times. Things became worse between herself and her husband — he seemed to be drunk all the time. The last straw was when Ann found that she was pregnant again. She felt that she was going mad and four months into pregnancy she decided to go for counselling. Ann clearly had a great deal of work to do on the sexual abuse. However, her immediate problem with her husband and her new pregnancy were far more prominent in her mind. After several counselling sessions, Ann decided that her priority for now was to sort out her present situation. She could not cope with the added emotional upheaval of dealing with her sexual abuse. She also felt that she would have no support from her husband.

Ann was put in touch with a social worker who helped to support her through the pregnancy and also contacted a marital counsellor. Nine months later she returned for counselling. She had had her baby and separated from her husband. She felt much more in control and ready to deal with the sexual abuse at this point. Ann may or may not go back to her husband, that is a decision for the future. At present she is looking after herself and is in a stable position to do so.

This chapter is intended primarily for anyone who is considering going for counselling. We outline the kinds of issues and questions that have to be thought about carefully, before you decide to go ahead. Counselling at any time is not easy and, given the nature of sexual abuse and the damage it causes, it is clearly not a decision to be taken lightly. When you are triggered by something in your life and realise that perhaps this is something that you have to deal with, it is important to understand what lies ahead. No one likes to fail and if you start counselling and do not see it through, you may feel worse than you did when you started. No one wants this to happen, so it is important to work it out first.

What does counselling involve? Basically, counselling offers a way of becoming free of the painful and damaging effects of sexual abuse. It can be a promise of hope and of a new and better life. It can enable women who have been abused to find real peace and freedom from pain, sadness and despair. Counselling is a slow journey, taking anything from six months to a year, sometimes even longer. As well as time it takes courage and patience. It is a painful experience because there is so much hurt around sexual abuse. Essentially, counselling involves looking at the abuse, which means having to face that pain. In the beginning, this can be hard to understand for those who have spent most of their time trying to forget, trying not to feel. In counselling, they are asked to remember and to feel. The reason for this is that the only way to be free of sexual abuse is to confront it, to talk about it, to tell all the secrets surrounding it.

The first thing to consider is whether this is a good time for you to start. As we have said, counselling is a painful process in which you may have to take a hard look at yourself, your relationships and your life in general. You will be reviving memories and feelings which you have been avoiding for some time, perhaps quite a long time. There will be good and bad days during this process. There will be times when you may feel very low indeed. Without doubt, this is going to disrupt your daily routine, and your attention and concentration will probably not be as sharp as usual. You will not fall apart, but you will feel fragile for a time. This must be considered seriously, as it is an unavoidable part of the counselling process. If you are not prepared to accept disruption you cannot expect to be successful in your counselling. So, it is really about you giving yourself permission to take time to look after yourself.

Other people and areas of your life may have to be put on hold for a while, as you concentrate on yourself. You must work out whether this is really possible in your present situation. Take a look at what is happening at home and at work. Are there people or situations that need your full attention and energy at the moment? Is there some crisis which may be as much as you can cope with for now? Try to be very honest with yourself. Since there will probably be a part of you that does not want to look at the abuse at all, you may well be looking for obstacles and excuses. Some things are fairly permanent, such as having two children and trying to hold down a paid job. These situations are not going to disappear, but are not impossible to get around. You may not function at your most efficiently for a few months, but that is not the end of the world. You will probably be more efficient once it is over. Other situations, such as your relationship breaking up or being pregnant, may be enough for you to handle for now. In this case, it would be better for you to wait a couple of months before you start. It is also important that you feel well physically and are not run down or dealing with an illness. You will need your energy for counselling.

If you are on medication it may be a hindrance, depending on what kind and how much medication you are taking. Many women have been using tranquillisers or anti-depressants for a long time and this can blunt feelings or reactions. You may need to stop your medication first and then proceed to counselling. Of course if you have to come off medication, you should do so only under your doctor's supervision.

Once you have decided the time is as right as it can be, the next step is to take stock of the kind of support that you have outside the counselling situation. You will need someone whom you can trust and talk to openly. There are going to be some rough times and it is important to be able to share this with someone. You may know immediately who this person is, but for some women it may be harder to find the right person. Do not give up and think that there is no one. If you think carefully there is always someone. The person you choose may not always know the right thing to do or say, but they should be able to listen. Telling someone outside the counselling area is important, as it helps to make it more real for you. Someone else knows and believes you. It may be someone close to you, or someone you feel will understand. Keep looking, there is bound to be someone whose support you can call on.

Perhaps the hardest part is to come to terms with the fact that you yourself have to do all the work. Your counsellor can help, lead the way, explain what is happening, but she cannot do all the work for you. You will have to do the remembering, feel all the emotions, make the changes and battle your way to the end of it. There is no magic wand or sugar-coated pill that will do the job for you. There are no easy answers, and although you may get angry with your counsellor, you must keep reminding yourself that she can help you through. You must take responsibility for your own counselling, look for what you need, ask for what you want, but in the end it is up to you.

You need a strong commitment to go through the process. Once you have started, you have already changed something, so if you give up halfway through, things will not go back to the way that they were before you started counselling. There comes a stage in every counselling process when you probably feel like running away and forgetting all about it. However, if you run at this stage, you will be stuck with it. You have taken the problem out of the hiding-hole and it just will not go back in. If you start, you must promise yourself that you are going to finish. You may have to face things that you do not want to face, and make changes that are very hard to make, see things in a different way. You will probably feel differently about yourself, your relationships, the way you are living and the life style you lead. You have to be prepared to take these things in your stride and believe that at the end of it, you will know where everything fits and belongs. This means that you have to work between sessions. It is not enough to come to your counsellor every week or fortnight and forget all about it in the times between each session. It is your work. You must persevere until it is finished.

What you need most, and if you have survived sexual abuse you will have plenty of it, is courage. It takes courage from the moment you begin to think, 'maybe I need to work this out', right through to the very end. It takes courage to believe that you can work it out and that you have the right to do so. It takes great courage to face ourselves as we really are. If you have got to the point where you are reading this book or thinking of going for help, there is a part of you that is ready to confront it. It is the part of you that has never given up, that has always believed and hoped that things should and could be better. It is the part that believes you have the right to be happy, the part that has been untouched by the abuse and has helped you to survive up until now. Trust this deep and very strong part of yourself and go forward. Your courage and determination will lead you where you want to go.

CHAPTER 5

THE PATH OF SELF-DISCOVERY

PAUL-ANN

Paul-Ann is twenty-three years old. She is the second of four daughters. She lives on her own in a flat three miles from her family home. Her father has been in England for the past eight months. Paul-Ann's mother will not speak to her and will not allow her to visit home, but some of her sisters come to visit her. Apart from that, she lives a lonely, quiet life; she works hard at her job as a receptionist, but rarely socialises with anyone. Paul-Ann has little or no self-confidence.

Paul-Ann's father is an alcoholic, but despite that, he managed to build up a thriving practice as a solicitor. He was well-known, well-liked and although he 'drank heavily', he was conscientious and thorough in his work. The family lived in a beautiful house, the children were always well dressed, well cared-for and did well in school.

When Paul-Ann was thirteen years old, her father came into her bedroom late one night and raped her savagely and quickly. She tried to scream, but he stuffed a hanky in her mouth and warned her that he would kill her if she made a sound. The next day, Paul-Ann put the blood-stained sheets in the washing machine and told her mother that she had started a period. This was the start of a nine year nightmare for her. Over the years Paul-Ann's father forced her to co-operate in many of his perverse sexual fantasies. She had to dress up for him, read pornographic stories to him and engage in various other degrading sexual activities. He frequently threatened her and often hurt her. Most of this happened on evenings when her mother played bridge. He gained and maintained a huge hold over Paul-Ann by threatening that he would start to abuse her younger sisters, if she did not co-operate. She could not bear the idea of this happening. The thought of his doing to any of them what he did to her made her physically sick. People could not understand why she did not leave, but how could she leave her younger sisters vulnerable to him?

Ten months ago, Paul-Ann came home one night to find her father in bed with her sixteen-year-old sister Lynn. She went cold with shock and fear. The next day, she questioned her sister only to find that her father had been abusing her for two years. Worse was to come — she discovered that he was also raping her fourteen-year-old sister Kate. Something snapped in Paul-Ann. When she confronted her father, he tried to kill her by pushing her head into a sink full of water. She escaped and the next day reported him to the police and a social worker. Within six weeks, her father had been charged, and subsequently he left the country.

One of the most difficult parts of Paul-Ann's story is that her mother totally rejected her because of what she did. Her mother blames her for breaking up a 'good' family, for telling lies and for brainwashing her sisters. Sometimes, Paul-Ann wakes in the middle of the night and tries to imagine that it was all a bad dream, that she would wake up and find the mother and father that she once knew and loved as a child, oh, so long ago.

Lost Childhood

Counselling is really a journey back to childhood to try and repair the damage that was done. Inside every abused person there is a hurt child waiting for the right time to tell its secrets. That child is often unhappy, confused, angry or ashamed. Women who come for counselling can heal themselves, but to do that they need to get to know the child they once were, and allow themselves to feel what she felt.

A lost childhood cannot be regained; this is one of the saddest realities that abused women have to face. However, a hurt child can be healed, even many years after the abuse. The aim of counselling is to enable each person to achieve that for herself. It is a slow process and there are many different kinds of work involved in the different stages of counselling. In many ways, it is like peeling away the layers of an onion. Once you allow yourself to remember and to feel, other memories and feelings gradually emerge and these in turn will lead the way to further layers.

Telling and Remembering

The first stage in counselling involves remembering and telling what has happened. It is difficult to talk about sexual abuse, but it is very important to tell in detail what has happened, to express it as fully as possible to someone else. Women often feel that they could not possibly talk about the abuse, and especially women who have been subjected to very degrading sexual perversions and activities, eg abuse with an animal, or objects like knives. You need to remember that your counsellor will be open and accepting of everything that you may tell and that you are not the first or the only person to talk to her in this way. Any feelings which are held back prevent healing from taking place.

By the time women come for counselling they usually have some specific memories to relate. Once women start to talk about what has happened to them, other memories will emerge, other times, places and other ways in which they were abused. Once you give yourself permission to tell what has been buried for a long time, it begins to come slowly to the surface.

It happens that women have come to talk about being abused by one person, eg a babysitter, but then discover in the course of counselling that they were also abused by someone else, eg a brother. It frequently happens that they have come to deal with a particular type of abuse, eg fondling and touching, only to discover that there was further serious abuse involved, inter-course/oral or both. Women are often afraid of what else they are going to uncover and this is usual and natural. We believe that this remembering occurs because it is the right time, it is safe now to remember because there is a way of coping with the abuse. The most painful abuse is usually buried the deepest and may only emerge after some time in counselling. There is often disbelief about what is being uncovered, especially if the abuse is buried so deeply that you had no idea it had ever happened.

In the beginning the memories may seem quite unreal. Having spent most of your life trying to forget something which, when it appears, brings a sense of unreality, people often ask themselves, 'am I making this up?' And there may be a large part of them that does not want to believe that this abuse happened because it is so painful.

In our experience, our memories rarely betray us. We may fight the truth for days or weeks, but in the end we accept it because in our hearts we know it fits. Women often bargain with themselves at this stage; 'I will accept that I was sexually abused at five years of age, but I will not accept that I was sexually abused at three years of age'. Sometimes the bargaining can go on for weeks, as they try to fight the truth. This can be a miserable time for women in counselling, often they want to leave and to stop it all, but with courage and support, it is posible to face the unbearable.

Sometimes women become very stuck in their remembering. A woman might have a strong sense that her brother abused her and yet have no specific memories to match the feelings. She tries and tries to remember and then says, 'No, it cannot be true because I do not remember'. Usually when this happens, it is again about bargaining, about not really wanting to face this particular part of the abuse. Sometimes remembering occurs through dreams which can be very vivid and symbolic. Most women know when their dreams are connected to the abuse and can use these dreams to make further progress in counselling.

Feelings and Emotions

Often after a first session in counselling, a woman says 'Well, I have told you everything. Now what do I do?'. Remembering and disclosing are only the first stage of the whole healing process. The hardest part of counselling is to allow yourself to feel all the emotions that got buried with the abuse.

There is no short cut through this work. You cannot decide to block the rest. This 'feeling' stage is often a very confusing time for women in therapy and they frequently say, 'I felt bad before I started this, but I feel ten times worse now'. In a sense that is true, yet the only way to become free of the pain is to experience it, and counselling in the first place is because the price of burying that pain has become too high.

We live in a society where people are discouraged from sharing any kind of strong feelings. We do not cry in public, we do not express our anger, we do not allow ourselves to feel depressed or sad for any length of time, and if we do, we begin to think that we are not 'normal', that something is seriously amiss. One of the first things to be learned in counselling for sexual abuse is that it is normal and healthy to have feelings. Some women are afraid of 'cracking up' or going mad when this starts to happen.

In counselling, women are encouraged to express their feelings in safe and appropriate ways. This may well mean going through long bouts of sadness and depression, with many painful tears. This is a typical reaction to sexual abuse. Allowing yourself to feel the sadness of abuse is allowing yourself to feel the loneliness and pain of that abuse, the misery that surrounds it, the despair and emptiness of it. These feelings can be repressed for many years, and women can experience a great sense of relief in being able to finally let go. Many tears may be shed, but they are healing tears. Women are never asked to cope with more than they can bear, and counsellors will always provide safety and support for the women they are working with.

Anger is another feeling common with sexual abuse. The anger is often felt towards the abuser, but can also be experienced towards other people. Parents, particularly mothers, are the targets for a lot of anger, anger that they did not see or recognise what was going on and prevent the abuse from happening. Sometimes women feel angry at what has been taken from them, innocence, happiness, a lost childhood. In counselling, women are encouraged to get in touch with their anger and are helped to do so, in a safe and constructive way. This can be difficult to do initially as women are generally discouraged from expressing anger in our society.

There is also the fear of losing control, although this rarely happens when anger is dealt with responsibly. Repressed anger can do far more damage to a person than expressed anger. Releasing repressed anger can generate a lot of energy and give victims a sense of power and control over their lives again.

Anger can even be a way through to forgiveness. It is possible for some women who have suffered sexual abuse to forgive their abusers. This does not always happen, and we want to stress that it is not an essential part of therapy. But there are many women who, despite the fact that they hated the abuse, still love their abuser. It is important to acknowledge and feel the anger, but it may be possible to forgive. This may be easier in cases where the abuser is willing to take responsibility for what he has done.

There are other emotions to be dealt with in the process of counselling. Fear runs throughout the process. Fear of remembering more, fear of painful feelings of fear of falling apart. Again, this is quite typical. There is no rule that says that you must never be afraid. Just because you are frightened of something does not mean that it cannot be faced. Any woman who survives sexual abuse is already strong because she has survived. This strength will emerge more and more as counselling progresses.

Many women who have been abused feel guilty and ashamed of the abuse. They blame themselves for not stopping the abuse for not telling somebody, for 'letting' it happen to them. Often, the abuser will feed into this guilt by telling the child that she is to blame, that she made him do these things. If bribery has been a part of the abuse, a child can feel that she has traded herself and that she is somehow responsible. All of these feelings have to be faced and worked through. The abuser is always responsible for sexual abuse, never the child, no matter what the child does. Perhaps one of the most difficult things for a woman to face in counselling is the realisation that there was an element of pleasure in the sexual abuse, either because she welcomed the cuddles and physical contact that went along with it, or became sexually aroused. If sexual abuse persists over a period of time, it is common for children to become confused about this and to feel that they took part in and were responsible for the abuse, but this is not the case. Women who become sexually aroused within an abusive relationship are even more trapped within the whole secrecy of abuse. In a sense they are more inclined to lay guilt on themselves instead of on the abuser.

There is a lot of work to be done in counselling and each piece of work that you do, each layer that is uncovered will lead to another layer, until finally all of the truth is told and all of the feelings shared. But counselling is not just about pain and hardship; it is essentially a time of hope. Many women speak of being free and feeling free for the first time in their lives. No one can ever understand or estimate how precious that freedom is for someone who was trapped and burdened for many years. Counselling does not bring with it the promise of total happiness. There will always be issues and situations in your life that can cause pain. Nor does it offer the possibility of being able to forget all about the abuse. What it offers, very importantly, is the ability to be able to accept the abuse, and live with it as part of your life. You will never forget your abuse, but you will remember it with less acute pain.

CHAPTER 6

ISSUES YOU MAY ENCOUNTER

SIOBHAN

Siobhan has had counselling for six months. She is twenty-two years of age and originally came to deal with abuse by an uncle, when she was approximately ten or eleven. She had fairly clear memories of the abuse and seemed to be working through it well. However, after several sessions, she seemed to reach an impasse. There seemed nothing else for her to tell and yet she was in a constant state of fear. Siobhan felt as if something terrible was going to happen.

On looking more closely at her feelings and delving deeper into her childhood, Siobhan discovered that she had also been abused by her father. This was at a younger age, and she had to confront the fact that her father had been abusing her as far back as she could go. Her first memories were of approximately six months old. Of course, this raised the question of her mother's role. Siobhan clearly remembered incidents where her mother had ignored the abuse. She had to re-live the awful desperation of her early childhood. Fortunately, Siobhan's father had died when she was six and so the abuse ended.

Siobhan worked through many of these feelings with great difficulty and pain, but suddenly found herself panicking again. It seemed that there was more. It finally emerged that she had been abused by an older brother from the age of twelve to fifteen years. This particular abuse seemed no less traumatic than the previous abuse she had dealt with. Why then the difficulty in recalling it? Why was it the most deeply buried?

Gradually, haltingly, it came to the surface. When Siobhan was abused by her brother, she had responded physically. She enjoyed it, sometimes she had even sought it out. Siobhan was fond of her older brother, he was nice to her. She even imagined the two of them caught up in a romantic entanglement. At fifteen, she stopped it, horrified when the dream-world started to fade. The only way to deal with the guilt and shame was to forget it.

Siobhan is now rapidly making progress towards recovery. It seems a far cry from the abuse that she first acknowledged, but her survival instinct was at work. She came with what was the easiest part for her and then battled on to the end. It is important for us to realise the difference there may be between what appears to be the worst (most difficult) part in acknowledging abuse, and what a woman who has been abused actually feels and remembers.

In looking at the process involved in counselling, we have seen that there are many different issues and emotions to deal with. In this chapter, we want to look at some of the specific issues which may have to be dealt with, often the most difficult and therefore the most deeply buried. Typically they emerge late in the counselling process and can be terribly painful to face. However, if any of these is an issue for you, it must be looked at, or that sense of freedom may still elude you, just out of reach. Nothing in your abuse is new, it has happened before to other women. Although it may seem unbelievable and unspeakable to you, remember that your counsellor knows that with sexual abuse, anything is possible. You need to shed yourself of it — this must be your absolute priority.

MOTHERS

An issue that emerges for everyone at some point in their counselling is 'mother'. The role of your mother actually cannot be avoided if you are to look fully at your abuse. If abuse by your mother is what brought you to counselling, then you are confronting it from the very beginning, although you may be very slow to admit your feelings about her. For all women our feelings about our mothers are deep and very complex. Our sense of loyalty and love is very strong where our mothers are concerned. It can feel unbearable to see any wrong in her or admit that she has failed us in any way. We are all brought up with the idea that we must love our mothers and that even if no one else cares about us, mother always does. There are problems with this on a lot of levels.

The first is that we do not always love our mothers. Some women hate their mothers, some love her because she is 'mum', but do not like her very much as a person. Some do love her very much, but can be let down by her or feel unloved by her. Many women have very confused and ambivalent feelings about their mothers, but feel that this is not natural and therefore must never be admitted. Other women feel very protective about their mothers and so cannot allow themselves to say or even think anything bad about her.

A further problem with this presumed loving bond between mothers and their children is the tremendous pressure it puts on the mother herself. Society, our culture and indeed women themselves put enormous demands and pressures on her to be perfect. She must love all of her children equally and always put her children first. She must always do everything 'right' and above all, must know everything about her children. If something goes wrong, she 'should' know instinctively and know exactly how to put everything right. It is little wonder that so many mothers cannot fulfill such impossible expectations. In the course of their counselling, most women will inevitably face the question, 'Did my mother know?'. It is usually of crucial importance to the woman and for many, it can become the burning issue. They have to find out, it can become the difference between recovery and continuing pain. The obvious solution would be to ask her, presuming she is still alive. However, this does not usually prove to be so easy. Most mothers will say that they did not know about the abuse, which may or may not be the case. Denial is a theme that runs through sexual abuse — for abusers, those who are abused, and others involved. Denial by mothers is not an issue that can be dealt with here in detail. Clearly it happens for many complex reasons. Hearing your mother's denial may bring you no closer to peace. The reality for most women is that they already know the answer to this question somewhere deep inside themselves. In searching and examining memories and feelings, they will confirm this.

The problem centres on facing the answer. If a woman comes to the conclusion that her mother did not know and could not have known of the abuse, there is great relief. However, there may well be other feelings relating to our expectations of our mother. The woman may feel great anger about why she did not know, or did not realise that something was wrong. Her mother, she feels, should have known and protected her child better. These feelings are very real and must be worked through. Remember that you can love someone very much and still be very angry with them. However, if you realise that indeed your mother did know or, more difficult still, was actively involved in the abuse, the pain can be devastating. It goes against every rule we have been led to believe in. Unfortunately, this is the reality many women have to face. Again, the reasons for a mother participating in, or ignoring, the abuse are varied and complex, but are not our concern here. The feelings of pain, hatred and anger that women have to deal with, when confronting their mother's knowledge of or participation in the abuse, is intense and often far greater than the feelings towards the abuser.

The total lack of protection, hopelessness and feelings of being unloved are all re-lived. Acceptance when it comes does so slowly and painfully. Part of this acceptance is probably the loss of all illusion around this perfect, loving mother who would have saved them, had she known. Women who find that their mother participated in the abuse have to confront an even greater sense of betrayal and often have had to face worse abuse. When a mother is involved, there is no fear of detection and often the abuse can be very severe. Discoveries of this kind are very frightening and will probably make you feel that you are better off not knowing. We can only say again that a part of you does know and is struggling with it all the time. Once you face it, acceptance does come, and the struggle with your own fear and memory will be over.

SECRETS

Another issue that is very important for some women, and again very deeply buried, is that of extremely perverted or sadistic sex. Many women who have been subjected to this may feel that they can never tell their experiences. It is deeply repressed, yet enormously influences the way that they feel about themselves. Again, it must be told and once again, we repeat, it has happened to others.

The kind of abuse that we are referring to may include being forced to have sexual contact with animals, whether oral sex or intercourse. Dogs are especially common in this kind of abuse, although other animals may be used. Being tied up or beaten or having to beat or tie the abuser; being abused by two or more men at the same time, eg one man having intercourse with you while at the same time the other man has oral sex with you; the use of implements such as knives, sticks, bottles and stones. Many women have been penetrated with a variety of objects during oral, vaginal and anal sex.

Cigarettes or matches have been used to burn the woman anywhere on her body, including the genitals. Some women are urinated or defecated upon or have to do the same to the abuser. Some abusers have made their victims eat their own faeces or that of the abuser. The abuser can ejaculate somewhere on the body of their victim including the face, mouth or hair. Some abusers actually mutilate the body of the woman by cutting or burning them. When this happens frequently or is especially severe, the woman may be left with obvious physical scars.

These are some examples of the kinds of abuse suffered by women. It is not meant to include everything and the human imagination is far-ranging. Where abuse has been long term, often it becomes progressively worse as the abuser gets bored doing the same thing, although for some women, the abuse may have been very severe from the beginning.

Some abusers act out all their fantasies from the start of the abuse. Abuse of this kind leaves particularly deep emotional scars, which can lead to especially self-destructive tendencies. Some victims may continue to mutilate themselves or to allow people to abuse them. It is important that you do not hide any of these effects; they do not mean that you are weird, sick or perverted. It is a measure of the damage that has been done to you and, as a result, of how bad you feel about yourself. Most women who have been abused in these ways describe feelings such as being 'half human', feeling like 'a piece of shit', 'degraded', and so dirty that they will never be clean. It is vital to remember that these things have been done to you, they are not you. The motive for this kind of abuse is to degrade and humiliate you. It can also be worked through. *You are a person of value and worth, you are not going to be defeated.*

CONFLICTING FEELINGS: LOVING THE ABUSER

Another issue that we want to look at is that of loving the abuser or trading with him. Many women feel they have loved and still do love their abuser, which can lead to a great deal of conflict. For instance, you can feel that you have no right to love this person, that others will think you strange if you do, but for many women the only attention they got as children was from their abuser. This may have been the person to whom you were the closest, and this is crucially important for you to acknowledge. On the other hand, it may be very hard to accept that you were abused by this person because you feel he loved you and you loved him. Admission can feel like a huge betrayal of yourself and of him. In recognising the abuse, your feelings towards this person may alter, a very painful and frightening experience. You may have to face the fact that this person did not love you the way you imagined. You may need to acknowledge that you traded sex for what you thought were love and affection and that this was the only way you could get any love at the time. It can seem like a fair exchange and if this was the only way open to you to feel loved, that exchange is perfectly understandable. We all need to feel loved and the person in the wrong is the abuser who takes advantage of this need. Do not be afraid to say that you still love this person. You are entitled to your own feelings. We can often love people and yet hate what they have done to us. It is important to acknowledge the damage they have done, but you are not obliged to hate them.

RESPONDING TO THE ABUSE

An issue for many women is the fear of having sexually responded during the abuse. As a young child, your body may have enjoyed all the attention it was getting. It is a natural reaction to experience physical pleasure if touched in a sexually arousing way, and this is more likely to happen if you are not afraid of your abuser. Abuse which was performed in a playful, gentle, even affectionate guise may well carry with it recollections of quite pleasurable feelings for you.

As teenagers, many women remember responding strongly to the abuse. This is more likely to occur if, as we've said, the abuse is not violent or painful or frightening in any way. Many women recall a certain satisfaction at getting something out of it for themselves: 'If it is going to happen anyway, why not get some enjoyment out of it?'. Women who have been systematically violated over a long period of time may regard their abuse as routine, and your body is not going to realise that the wrong person is touching it.

Women often feel that if they ever responded physically at all they have no right to call it abuse. Look back to the definition of abuse. The adult is the one who has taken advantage of the situation and of your body. If he was not touching you, you would not be responding. He is the one who has broken the rules; you have not. He is the one responsible; you are not. Your only concern is to acknowledge how you feel about it.

ABUSE OVER A LONG PERIOD

Another painful issue for women is the timespan of the abuse. Many come for counselling believing that they were abused for perhaps a few months or a few years. In the course of counselling, months can change to years and a few years can extend to even longer periods of time. Your mind may have become blocked in order to make the abuse more acceptable. A lot of women have to face the fact that they were abused as babies and this can be a devastating realisation. It is so shocking and so unbelievable: how could anyone abuse a baby? Abuse of a baby often includes oral sex and this again seems too horrifying to believe. The memory is usually deeply buried and as it surfaces, slowly but surely, you may feel as if you are going completely mad. It can feel as if you have heard it somewhere or fantasised it. It is very painful for women to realise that there was never a time when they were not being abused.

44

If you have been abused from such a young age you have no natural defences to save you, there seems to be no alternative. It is then quite possible that the abuse may have continued right through teens and possibly into adulthood. It may also have made it much simpler for you to have been abused by many people. You may have had no sense of your own body and therefore allowed anyone to do what they wanted with it. Abuse by many people becomes especially repressed and someone who comes for counselling about abuse by one person may find that they were abused by several others. If you discover that you were abused by many people at a young age, you may feel that you were far happier never knowing. However, these feelings and this knowledge have to surface before you can understand who you are and why these things have happened to you. You cannot have full freedom without full knowledge. So, although it is undeniably painful, the truth of your abuse must be accepted. Most women who have had to confront their abuse and the extent of it also have a sense of reaching the end of it. The truth seems to answer all their questions about themselves and can make sense of their lives and their image of themselves. It brings a sense of release, the struggle to barricade the memories is over.

There are many other issues which emerge in counselling for women. If your particular concern or horror is not mentioned, do not be alarmed. It really would be impossible for us to cover everything here. The important thing for you to remember is that you need to tell everything. Don't waste your own time and energy picking out what you think is acceptable for others. You are the one who has been hurt and you are the one who must be healed. It is not your job to worry about your counsellor or agonise over her perception of you. You are probably your own harshest judge. You have survived so far, do not be afraid to heal yourself.

INCEST

When the burden seems too heavy
And life won't just chug along
Then you must look inside yourself
To find out what went wrong

If someone caused you damage
By a most unholy deed
The healing road is long and narrow
But it can give you what you need

I travelled down that lonely road
And searched the corners of my mind
But when I looked and dealt with it
It could be left behind

So now my life I've built again
Stronger, surer, true
No one would have thought that had happened to me
Might it have happened to you?

Who do you think is the loser
In that game of take and take?
Not I, who was the victim,
But he who chose to take

Now I know that I'm the winner
And I've triumphed over him
I can say I really know who I am
Can anyone say it for him?

Lilian Chambers, 1988

CHAPTER 7

RECOVERY

The road to recovery is long, hard and seemingly endless but there is light at the end of the tunnel. And this chapter deals with some issues which play a crucial role in reaching this light.

Many women in counselling say that they could or would never confront their abuser. By the end of counselling, not confronting may be equally impossible. There can be a strong urge to go back to the person who abused you and let him know that you remember everything, and how you feel about it. It may be necessary for you to confront your mother or your whole family — this is a personal decision and one which only you can make. Never allow yourself to be bullied into a confrontation if you aren't ready or feel that it is not necessary for you. It is also vital that you are in control of yourself and the situation. Even though initially you may be so angry that you want to run off and kill him, wait until you are sure of yourself, of what you are doing and why you are doing it.

The reasons for confrontation are many and varied and each woman has her own. The point of the exercise is to help you in your recovery. The idea is not to get answers from the abuser or admissions of guilt, apologies or understanding. It is unlikely that you will get any of these and they should not be your priority. Your priority is you and what you need to say.

In confronting your abuser you will be facing a reality which you have never come to grips with until now. Above all else you are demonstrating loudly and clearly your refusal to be silenced any longer. You may have been made to carry this secret for most of your life — but not anymore. The abuser's days of power are over, your days have begun. You have a voice and you intend using it. In breaking the silence, you are laying the blame where it belongs. It is no longer 'your' secret, you are handing back the guilt, shame and responsibility for the abuse to the person who is responsible for it. It is his to carry from now on.

Reactions differ after a confrontation. Some women feel elated and powerful for the first time in their lives, freed of the burden that they have been carrying. They have timed it well, they are finished. Others experience profound sadness and pain as they realise that, 'Yes, it is all really true'.

Confrontation always moves you closer to the end. It is a giant step towards recovery and although there may be a lingering hope that you were imagining things, recognition of the truth can bring with it a sense of release. The burden has been returned to the rightful owner and you are free.

Forgiveness is another issue that arises towards the end of your counselling. Can you, should you, forgive or not? Most of us have been brought up to believe that we must forgive those who hurt us, that it is the 'right' thing to do. Some people find that they can forgive, while others cannot or will not do so. No one ever has the right to tell you that you must forgive. For many who might otherwise be very forgiving people, incest is too great a crime ever to be forgiven. It is important to remember that forgiveness is not about condoning the abuse. If you can forgive, do so, not because you ought to or because you believe it will make you a 'better' person, but because forgiving can relieve you of the bitterness. For those who can forgive, there may be a feeling of leaving the experience behind forever, not forgotten, because it will never be forgotten, but unloaded. Some of you may forgive later, in your own time, and that is your right. But do not feel that you must. Only you know what you can and cannot do. And you must do it in your own way.

So it looks like you are on your way. However, just to keep you and your feet on the ground a little, it is important for you to realise that although this may be the end of your counselling, it is not the end of the work. From now on, you are healed sufficiently to continue alone, but there is business to finish, there are changes to be made and this can be very frightening.

Your marriage or relationship may well have suffered in the course of the upheaval your counselling has caused. You have changed as a person and this will inevitably affect any relationship in which you are involved. Sometimes it is fine and your partner may welcome the newly confident, assertive, loving you, but this will not necessarily be the case. You may no longer be happy with the relationship, but these patterns can be hard to shift. The way you have sex may need to alter. Perhaps you want to get a job or return to study, who knows?

It can happen and does happen that relationships change after counselling. This could be the best thing that ever happened to you, or it may be the reverse. Some relationships cannot survive a huge change in one partner where the other cannot adapt. An inability to change may indicate a problem in the relationship. However, more often, the change can be dealt with although this can be difficult and painstakingly slow. You may need counselling to help you both through the transition. But it can be done and for both of you, the relationship may be better than ever as you begin to feel more positive.

Through your counselling, you will very possibly have developed a deeper, clearer sense of your needs, your hopes and expectations. Do not be afraid to go after what you want in life. You are entitled to seek happiness. Do not expect disaster at every turn — that is the old you. Although your life will not suddenly become wonderful because you have dealt with your sexual abuse, your new sense of yourself will help you to start making the changes necessary for you to be happy. Remember, if you have got this far, you can do so much more. There will of course be ups and downs, but you have proved that you can cope. You know that having descended to the very pits of despair, you can come back up again. Who could possibly stop you now, except yourself? So go on, admit your fear, but get out there, grasp life fully and be happy.

CHAPTER 8

SEXUALITY

Most women who have been sexually abused experience problems around sex and sexuality later on in their lives. These problems are experienced and expressed in a variety of different ways. Some women have difficulties from the time of the abuse, while others develop problems many years later. Because of the nature of sexual abuse there is a lot of healing to be done around the area of sexuality. This usually comes towards the end of counselling, when all the other issues have been looked at. The problems that women who have been abused may encounter in sexual relationships range from a total dislike of sex to difficulties with particular sexual practices. They may find it hard to become aroused or to enjoy sex at all. The inability to respond sexually may be rooted in fear, fear of being physically hurt, fear of reawakening memories of the abuse. Some women may deny themselves the right to ever enjoy sex, as a form of self-punishment. This often happens in cases where they responded sexually at the time of the abuse.

Many women have a great fear of penetration and this is entirely understandable if they have had to endure painful sexual intercourse at a young age. Most women who have been abused will have problems about being touched in a way that mirrors the abuse. For one woman it is stroking on the neck, for another, perhaps kissing or licking.

Oral sex can frequently be difficult if there has been oral abuse. In this case, as with all other sexual practices, women are encouraged to be honest and assertive about what they want and do not want sexually. It is likely that there will be certain practices that some women will never enjoy, and they must have the freedom to choose. Giving a woman back the right to say 'no' can often be the very freedom she needs, to be able to trust again. A percentage of women who have been abused will react in the opposite way and 'act out' sexually. They apparently enjoy sex, and seem to have no difficulties at all with it. They 'freely' give their bodies to anyone who wants them. Some women may even turn to prostitution. Such promiscuity masks a deep despair and self-hatred. The 'acting out' is part of a self-destructive urge. Because these women have been so deeply hurt, they continue to hurt themselves. They feel that their bodies are 'damaged goods', worthless and useless. Sometimes women may hurt themselves very deeply in this way by subjecting themselves to degrading sexual activities or by damaging their own bodies in some way — cutting, shaving and starving themselves or overeating to the point of obesity. This self-destruction has a lot to do with misdirected anger, anger that is turned inwards instead of being directed towards the abuser. Women who behave in this way have no sense of their own value because their sense of self-worth has been taken away with the abuse. This can be regained in counselling.

Sexual abuse can continue to affect women's sexuality in other ways. Fantasies about the abuse may occur when having sex with a partner or when masturbating — fantasies about being raped, about being powerless, about the abuser, even fantasies about animals, if they were used in the abuse. Such fantasies can be hard to understand and even harder to admit to. Women may be very frightened by their fantasies, especially when they think that no one else could possibly feel as they do, but this is not true. Fantasies like these are common and are understandable. Talking to your counsellor about them will help to set your mind at rest, and will enable you to work through your feelings about them. It is not unusual for those who have been abused to feel that they have been physically damaged and mutilated by the abuse, which can make them afraid of sex. There may be great reluctance to actually examine their bodies to see if what they fear is true. In counselling, women are encouraged to do this, and are often overwhelmed with relief to find that their bodies are still intact and undamaged. Of course, there are women whose bodies have been marked or mutilated in some way, but with gentleness and courage, they can face their bodies and slowly get to know them and reclaim them. In fact, reclaiming your body is a vital part of the healing work that has to be done. This involves learning about your body by first looking at it, then touching it. It includes taking proper care of your body, long baths, nourishing food, exercise, anything that helps to make you feel positive.

For some women who have been abused, there may be particular difficulties and fears around the area of sexual identity which need to be acknowledged and sensitively worked through. Prior to counselling, women may have chosen a heterosexual, celibate or lesbian lifestyle. If the choice was made through fear or lack of trust then it seldom brings real happiness. Towards the end of counselling, women are encouraged to explore their sexual identity and to make real choices for themselves about the way they choose to express their sexuality.

When women come for counselling they are encouraged to stop being sexually active while they are having counselling. The reason for this is that it becomes increasingly difficult to enjoy sex while working through abuse. For most women there is a great relief in not having to 'perform' for a period of time, particularly for those who have been participating in sex for years without ever really enjoying it. Towards the end of counselling, as women begin to feel good, they often feel the desire to have sex and to initiate it with their partners. It is the sense of control which makes the crucial difference for those who have been abused, the sense of genuinely being able to choose for themselves what they want. As with therapy, sexuality work cannot be rushed, it takes time to unlearn, it takes time to learn.

CHAPTER 9

HOPE

I am equal to all others and better than most
No one will ever control me again
I am like a newly born child watching
Listening and looking
At the brightest new world around me
It is finished
I am free

Maria, 1989

KAY'S STORY

I am a middle-aged woman with a family of two. Only last year, I discovered that I needed counselling for child sexual abuse. I always knew that it had happened because I was about eleven or twelve but I minimised it all of my life, thinking how lucky I was that I was not raped. It came up in counselling with my husband, who is an alcoholic. He too had raped me at the end of our relationship. It was the saddest and most painful experience of my life. Despite all the crises, and the hurtful put-downs over the years, we had had an enjoyable sex life. At the beginning of our married life, he was a caring lover, so we had time to get to know each other's bodies very well. That was before alcoholism reared its ugly head.

Looking back now, I know that sex was part of the pay-off for staying in a bad relationship. Deep deep down a part of me felt that I did not really deserve a good relationship. After all, I carried shame with me all of my life.

This kind of counselling is very tough, but very worthwhile. I have had the privilege of sharing my heart, soul and pain with caring counsellors and with some of the bravest women in the world. The honesty of those women bowled me over. I just had to get honest with myself. I could not sit there and not get into my feelings. For the first time in my life, I could be *me*. Whatever I said or felt, I was understood and accepted. We came from all walks of life, rich and poor. The one thing that we had in common was sexual abuse and that was all that mattered. Until the day I die, I will remember the bond that grew and grew between us over those months; the level of love and caring in that room will always stay in my heart. It will outweigh the hurt and the pain. I have changed quite a lot for the better. I am starting to love myself and intend to go on working on myself. I am not getting caught up in other people's problems, even though I care for them. I know from experience that the only way *out* is *through*. Sex will never be a pay-off for staying in a bad relationship.

I believe that I will be a stronger, wiser person, thanks to my counselling for sexual abuse. I will pray for those who abused me and let them go free — that way I will set myself free. My sincere thanks to the women survivors who helped me through.

JOAN'S STORY

My name is Joan. I am married with four children. I am thirty-five years of age and all my life I knew that I was different to other people. I was what everyone wanted me to be. I used to get very depressed and I would not know why, until last May when I discovered that I had been abused and raped by my father.

When I went for counselling, I was terrified of people and did not trust anyone. I could not even accept love from my husband or children. If anyone even liked me, I felt that there had to be a reason, as I felt that no one could like me for myself. I remember the first day that I met my counsellor. I remember telling her my story and the understanding and care that I sensed in her. Even though I was terrified, she made me feel that there was hope in my sad and empty life.

It took me a long time to open up to her, as I had become so protective of myself. It was so hard to trust her, to feel that she cared for me and to believe that I was a person, even though I felt like a broken heap. With help, love and understanding, I started to trust and to let people get to know me. I have been taught to like myself and even to love myself. As I sit and write this, I realise that I have come a long way since I decided to have counselling and when I finish, I know deep down inside that I will be a whole person. Some day.

If I had not got counselling I know that I would be walking through life with no hope or future. I would have taken my own life. But I know now that there is hope, I have a good future and I have the right to be happy and to be alive.

BRENDA'S STORY

My name is Brenda. I can remember when I was seven years of age, my father came to my bed and woke me up by putting his hand down my pyjamas and onto my private parts.

I hated it. I never knew what he was up to. He would say to me, 'You are the best little girl in the house. Never tell mammy. Your mammy would not like it if she knew.' My father would say to me that he would go to jail and my brothers and sisters would put me in a home. As I got older I was afraid to say anything to anybody. Around the age of fourteen, he brought me off in the car for a drive, or so he said.

We went to the beach where he stopped the car. I looked around, it was a lonely place. I was told to do as he said and say nothing.

I tried to push him off, but he was much bigger. I remember I was very sore after that. On the way home, I was told not to say a word to anyone. He did it to me a few times before I knew what he was up to. So then I stayed out of his way as much as I could. My father would say hurtful things like, 'You only want little boys, not me, your own father'. I hated my father for cheating on me. After all, I was his eldest daughter. He should have loved me by not touching me.

I met a guy and got married at the age of nineteen. When I was married a short while I became ill. I had two children then. I went down to eight and a half stone. I had been ten and a half. I could not eat. I had pains everywhere. I went to my doctor and he said that there was nothing wrong with me. One night, I became so ill that I ended up in hospital. I was in a bad way. The doctor asked my husband if anyone had done wrong to me.

'Someone', he told my husband, 'has done wrong to her and that's why she is behaving this way.' It was what my father had done. I had kept it a secret for too long, but who could I tell — not my mother nor my husband, who? I was still sick for a long time. When I would go to my mother's house, I was worse. I thought I was going mad. When I had my third child depression set in.

It was bad, I thought that it would pass, but it got worse. I joined the local ladies' club to get me out and about. They had a solicitor in one day talking about sexual abuse and counselling so I made a decision to seek help. Two weeks later I had an appointment. So, I started counselling.

It was hard work. I even told my mother and my husband about my father, something that I thought I would never do. My mother said that she knew there was something wrong.

She had an idea about my father but she supported him. She was on his side, making excuses. My husband and children need me and I them. We, as a family, lost out on so much over my father's greed. I would not have been able to get where I am today, but for counselling and meeting women like myself.

Every day life gets a little better. Sometimes I am sad. I would love to have had a father and mother who loved me. So I am going to do everything to make my home a happy one for my children. Children are people too. They need a loving home, someone to look up to and someone to love them.

RUTH'S STORY

My name is Ruth and I am thirty-nine years old, the mother of three children. My father was an alcoholic and a very violent man. I grew up hating him and being very frightened. My mother did the best she could but she never stood up to him. She died when I was sixteen and I became the mother in the home.

I met my husband when I was twenty and got married when I was twenty-two. I did not love my husband when we got married, but I was so afraid of my father and he had such an influence over me that I went ahead with it anyway. Within weeks, I realised that I had married an alcoholic. I have been unhappy for the past seventeen years. I have been abused by my husband in every way, he has beaten me, cursed me, humiliated me, cheated on me, blamed me, frightened me, deserted me but most of all he sexually abused me.

Now I am a married woman, an Irish Catholic, my own mother dead, three children and nowhere to go. On the surface I lived a very respectable normal life. No one would have suspected what was going on inside my hall door. Gradually, I became so distressed that I had to look for help. First for the alcoholism in my home and then realising that I had been sexually abused, I went for help for myself. I am a person. I have a right to make decisions for myself. The therapy has been very painful, there were times during the past few months that I would have preferred death to facing what I had to face, but with the care, love and support I am getting, I know that I will see this through as I can see how different my life is becoming. I have started to make decisions for myself about my life, I am beginning to feel so much better physically and I am looking better too.

I know that my happiness lies in my own hands and my willingness to go through with the therapy that I am being offered. I pray for the courage.

JULIA'S STORY

My name is Julia. I am thirty-eight years of age, I am married with five children. I was fifteen years married before I sought help. It was after my second daughter, my fourth child, that things started to emerge for me. From the time that Mary, my daughter, was about four years of age, I started to notice that she was very like me when I was young and somehow, I felt a very strong protectiveness towards her. I just knew that I had to mind her, but from what I did not know. When she was about six years old, a man that used to visit our house always liked to talk to Mary, and one day, I caught him with his hand down her pants. I nearly went mad, I screamed and roared and told him to get out. Suddenly, I was a small child again. I remembered the same thing had happened to me. After that I wanted to keep her by my side, I did not want to let her out or go to school but I had to let her go, and this caused me great distress.

Then other memories started to come, being abused while playing in the garden, being cornered in a shed, my brother locking me in a wardrobe. I felt so guilty about what had happened when I was small that I blamed myself completely. I thought that I would have to carry this burden, these awful secrets for the rest of my life.

My own relationship with my husband also changed. I had never really enjoyed making love, but I pretended that it was alright. After that incident with my daughter I did not want him coming near me at all and when I did give in to make love I felt as if it was not him I was making love to.

When he would fall asleep, I lay awake crying tears of sheer devastation, isolation and feeling guilty that I could not respond as a 'normal' wife. Of course, I blamed myself totally. I felt worthless, useless, I ceased to live, only to exist from day to day.

When I finally told a friend, she recommended that I go for counselling. I did not see how they could help me, but decided to give it a try, anything would be better than trying to live with my feelings of worthlessness, panic and fear. Going there was difficult, but the first thing to give me hope was that I was believed and accepted. I did not have to try to convince my counsellor that I was telling the truth, she knew through my pain and sadness that I was carrying an awful burden. Getting rid of my sense of blame gave me my first bit of peace. She told me that I was a small girl who had trusted adults and they had betrayed that trust. They were the ones who must carry the blame. I began to come alive, letting out feelings of inadequacy, hurt, anger and much sadness.

For months, every time I tried to talk about my childhood to my counsellor, I would cry. I often wondered would the day ever come that I would be able to talk without crying, and it did. It took some time before I could trust myself or my counsellor with all that I had to tell, because I was a child again, looking for reassurance and understanding that I had never had in my life before.

Over the last few months, I have been able to feel more and more that I am now beginning to have a sense of worth, I am seeing myself as a person who has a lot to give others and to myself not for what I can do, but for who I am. Sometimes I still have feelings of anger, sadness and regret. The strongest feeling I have is of being robbed of my childhood. I know that I cannot have my childhood back again, but taking it out and looking at it with the help of my counsellor has given me the freedom to look at my life now and see all the good things that I have. I know that I can go on, even though my life as a child, teenager and adult was overshadowed by those terrible events of sexual abuse. Through my counsellor and others with similar experiences to my own, I have come to recognise that these feelings of anger, sadness and regret are alright. They may surface in my life from time to time, but they will not have the same control over me. Every day, whether my days are good or bad, I am grateful that someone cared enough to give me a chance to know what freedom is. I say thanks to my friend who sent me there, thanks to my counsellor who helped me unwrap all that I never knew was inside me, wanting to get out. Lastly, I say thanks to myself for having the courage to take the risk. The risk was 'freedom' — the greatest gift that I could have for myself.

CHAPTER 10

WHAT HELP IS AVAILABLE - ADULTS AND TEENAGERS

We wish to stress that the counselling programme outlined in this handbook is specific to the Rape Crisis Centre in Dublin. We include below information regarding services that other agencies have stated they are offering. This is not a comprehensive list of all the help available, so check out other resources within your geographical area. There are a growing number of individual therapists working with sexual abuse victims so it is worth investigating these as well.

Belfast
Belfast Rape Crisis Centre/Sexual Abuse Resource Unit
41 Waring St
Belfast BT1 2DY
(080232) 249696
Peer service to adult women and girls. Individual counselling only, no group therapy. Counselling is non-directive, non-judgemental. Referral is self-referral. Service is free of charge.

Rape and Incest Line
105 University Street
Belfast BT7 1HP
(080232) 326803

Young People Centre
10 College Gardens
Belfast BT6 BQ
(080232) 661825

Clonmel

Clonmel Rape Crisis Centre,
14 Wellington Street
Clonmel, Co. Tipperary
(052) 24111

Counselling offered is non-directive peer counselling. Individual and group work is offered. Referral is self-referral only. Service is free of charge.

Cork

Cork Rape Crisis Centre
26 McCurtin Street
Cork
(021) 968086/968465

Dublin

CARI (Children At Risk in Ireland Foundation)
110 Lower Drumcondra Road
Dublin 9
(01) 308529

Multidisciplinary professional psychotherapy service for children and adolescents who have been sexually abused. This is a non-investigative, post-validation service for children up to eighteen years of age and their non-abusing family members. Support and advice is available. Referrals are through community care teams, GPs, psychologists, other agencies and schools.
Service is operated on a sliding scale of payment.

St John of God Community Psychiatric Service
Cluain Mhuire
Newtown Park Avenue
Blackrock
Co. Dublin
(01) 2800365

In Patient, Day Patient, and Out Patient psychiatric service for children, adolescents and adults. Referral is generally through the client's family doctor. Treatment is free for medical card holders within the catchment area. Individual therapy only.

The Children's Hospital
Temple Street
Dublin 1
(01) 8745214/8742887

Multidisciplinary professional and assessment service for children and families where child sexual abuse is suspected. The primary aim is to provide a validation service. Children up to sixteen years are seen at the unit. Some therapy is available for child victims, but there is no service for adult victims here. Referral from the North City only, is through Community Care Personnel, GPs, parents and Gardaí. The service is free of charge.

Our Lady's Children's Hospital
Crumlin
Dublin 12
(01) 558111

Multidisciplinary and professional service for children and families where child sexual abuse is suspected. The primary aim is to provide a validation service. Referrals are again through Community Care Personnel, GPs, parents and Gardaí. The catchment area is South City, Co. Kildare and Co. Wicklow. No charge.

Dublin Rape Crisis Centre
70 Lower Leeson Street
Dublin 2
(01) 6614911

The Dublin Rape Crisis Centre offers a professional therapy service to male and female adult and teenage victims of sexual abuse. Individual and group therapy is offered. The type of counselling offered is outlined in this handbook. Referral can be taken through other agencies or self-referral. Service is free of charge to those who cannot afford to pay but a sliding scale is operated for those who can pay.

Sexual Assault Treatment Unit
Rotunda Hospital
Dublin 1
(01) 8730000

Childline
Freephone 1-800-666666
10 a.m. to 10 p.m. for children in trouble.
This is a freephone number and may be dialled at no cost
from anywhere in Ireland.

Ennis

Our Lady's Hospital
Ennis
(065) 21414

Contact person: Clinical Psychologist. Professional service for
victims and perpetrators of sexual abuse. Individual work
only. Referral is through RCCs, GPs, Psychiatrists, Social
Workers and also self-referral. No charge.

Galway

Galway Rape Crisis Centre
3 St Augustine St
Galway
(091) 64983

Limerick

CARI (Children At Risk in Ireland Foundation)
29 Upper Mallow Street
Limerick
(061) 413331

Limerick Rape Crisis Centre
17 Upr Mallow Street
Limerick
(061) 311511

Counselling offered is non-directive peer counselling to
female and male victims of rape and child sexual abuse.
Referral is both self-referral and through other agencies.
Service is free of charge.

St Joseph's Hospital
Mulgrave Street
Limerick
(061) 46166

Contact person: Clinical Psychologist. Individual counselling to women and men. Referral is through GP. No charge for this service.

Sligo

Community Care Health Centre
Cleverage Road
Sligo
(071) 60222

Professional psychological service for victims of sexual abuse of all ages. Individual counselling only at present.

Wicklow

Irish Parents Together
c/o Health Centre
Glenside Road
Wicklow

For parents of sexually abused children.